Youth

Advice From Grand Ayatullah Sayyid Ali al-Sistani

Youth

The advice of His Eminence Grand
Ayatullah Sayyid Ali al-Sistani, the supreme
authority of Muslims, to the youth in response to
a request for counsel and guidance from a group of
socially active college students about their role
in society and what is required of them

I.M.A.M.

IMAM MAHDI ASSOCIATION OF MARJAEYA

Imam Mahdi Association of Marjaeya, Dearborn, MI 48124, www.imam-us.org
© 2017 by Imam Mahdi Association of Marjaeya
All rights reserved. Published 2017.
Printed in the United States of America

ISBN-13: 978-0-998-25443-2

Contents

Contents

I.M.A.M.'s Foreword

In the name of God,
the All-Beneficent, the All-Merciful

And may God's blessings be upon
Muhammad and his pure progeny

Apiece of advice coming straight from the heart can be immensely effective, particularly for those seeking direction on how to tread through this life. Guidance of this kind often takes its most potent form when relayed as a series of personal experiences and trials, as well as the lessons learned thereof, because it is a part of human nature to learn from the examples of others. This is even more the case when a wise person imparts what he or she has learned and acquired through personal effort and experience as opposed to mere theoretical suppositions and opinions. Now imagine the impact of advice shared by a person who occupies a lofty spiritual rank and a high religious post—as in being the representative of Imam al-Mahdi, may God hasten his return.

Dear young reader, what you have before you is advice—valuable and rare jewels coming from a person who possesses piety, knowledge, wisdom, and all the honorable traits one can aspire to. He is the supreme religious authority of Muslims, His Eminence Grand Ayatullah Sayyid Ali al-Husayni al-Sistani, may God prolong his life.[1]

The Importance of the Advice of Scholars

66 *I communicate to you the messages of my Lord, and I am your well-wisher, and I know from Allah what you do not know.*
(*Quran 7:62*) 99

Dominant personalities who possess unique skills and talents, and who are often well-known across the world, have the power and ability to strongly influence others either positively or negatively. The socially accepted images of these people, and sometimes they themselves, are used for commercial, economic, political, and other purposes to influence public opinion on various issues. Yet, even among these paragons, the

---

1. We felt it necessary to familiarize the reader with His Eminence. Thus, we have included a brief biography of him at the end of this booklet.

most influential people in any society remain the scholars, whose actions can profoundly move the masses. This is particularly true of religious and spiritual scholars because they represent a human state that is seen to be higher than that of the average man or woman, one that is completely unbiased and not swayed by any outside influence.

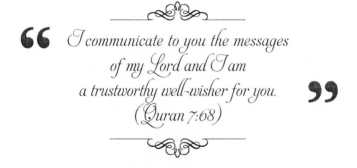

> *I communicate to you the messages of my Lord and I am a trustworthy well-wisher for you.*
> *(Quran 7:68)*

As such, one of the most important characteristics of good advice is that it must be given with the pure intention of obeying God, the Glorified, and not for the achievement of personal goals, or due to bias, personal interests, or factional (e.g., ethnic, tribe, etc.) politics. The Quran provides perfect examples of how to give advice and convey words of positivity and support. For instance, Prophet Noah (may peace be upon him) says to the people of his community, "I communicate to you the messages of my Lord, and **I am your well-wisher, and I know from Allah what you do not know**" (Quran 7:62). Similarly, the Quran also quotes Prophet Hud (may peace be upon him) who says, "I communicate to you the messages of my Lord and **I am a trustworthy**

well-wisher for you" (Quran 7:68). God even provided compassionate counselors to the prophets. For example, Khidr was a supporter, counselor, and teacher to Moses. In addition, the Holy Quran tells the story of a believer who was from the Pharaoh's people but in actuality was a supporter of Prophet Moses (may peace be upon him). In relation, the verse states, "and there came a man from the city outskirts, hurrying. He said, 'Moses! The elite are indeed conspiring to kill you. So leave. **I am indeed your well-wisher**'" (Quran 28:20).

Even after the time of Prophet Muhammad (may peace and blessings be upon him and his progeny), who was the seal of the prophets and messengers, the continuation of divine advice occurred through the words and actions of the holy imams[2] (may peace be upon them). These words and actions were narrated by *muhaddiths*[3] and collected so that they could serve as a written advice for humanity for the rest of time.

Consequently, the pious jurists of the time were directed by the holy imams to represent them, disseminate their

---

2. The holy imams were the twelve divinely appointed successors of Prophet Muhammad (pbuh), beginning with his cousin and son-in-law Ali ibn Abi Talib, then his grandsons al-Hassan and al-Hussain (sons of Ali and the Prophet's daughter Fatimah), and then nine more successively from father to son from the lineage of al-Hussain.

3. A *muhaddith* is a person who memorizes thousands of hadiths. Some muhaddiths have collected the hadiths they memorize in collections, such as *Al-kafi* by Shaykh Muhammad ibn Yaqub al-Kulayni (died 329 AH).

advice, and lead the believers. This was particularly crucial in the Age of Disappearance or after the occultation of Imam al-Mahdi (may God hasten his return). Since then, this select group of highly trusted jurists has carried on this tradition of giving advice for more than a millennium. Furthermore, we see that many jurists of the school of the progeny of the Prophet (may peace be upon them) have devoted a part of their time to giving advice and instruction to believers so that the latter can fulfill their responsibilities before God, the Glorified, and attain happiness during this life while simultaneously ensuring felicity in the afterlife.

The Importance of This Advice

This advice from Grand Ayatullah Sayyid al-Sistani (may God prolong his life) is an example of the eternal and weighty guidance provided by the jurists of the school of the progeny of the Prophet (may peace be upon them). Yet, this advice has special importance for several reasons, some of which are as follows.

IT COMES FROM A PRUDENT SCHOLAR who has exceeded eighty years of age, most of which was spent with books on various disciplines, experiencing life and its calamities, traveling to many countries, getting to know a great number of people, and raising a family and grandchildren, many of whom are themselves distinguished and exceptional figures in the community. Thus, this advice is the result of a profoundly successful and meaningful life, and as such it is an example that should be followed. It was not inspired by theories, abstract thoughts, or imagination as one might encounter in scientific instructional manuals or fictional novels, respectively.

THIS ADVICE COMES FROM A HIGH RELIGIOUS OFFICIAL. The religious authority is a jurist who possesses and has fulfilled all the requirements needed to issue religious edicts and who represents Imam al-Mahdi (may God hasten his return), the rightful successor of the Prophet (may God's blessings be upon him and his progeny). Any word that comes from a person of such stature and position has an impact that is incomparable. Therefore, this advice is not only a recommendation but a constitution and a road map that all young believers should implement and follow.

THESE COMMANDMENTS SPEAK TO THE YOUNG GENERATION as a whole with no exceptions, just as prophets spoke to all humans with no exceptions. Such has been the approach of the supreme religious authority in providing fatherly guidance and instruction because it serves this comprehensive role with respect to all believers without limits based on ethnicity, country, or social group. In fact, his message is intended for all of humanity.

IN ADDITION TO ALL OF THE ABOVE, HIS EMINENCE HAS FOCUSED THIS ADVICE ON SCIENTIFIC SPECIALTIES and the necessity for innovation and novel approaches. Furthermore, he has paid special attention to women's issues and the importance of social and familial institutions.

This advice should be used as a springboard and a road map by all young people who aspire to be successful in this life and in the hereafter. Most people go through a period of prodigality in their youth. Some even exaggerate their piety and abstemiousness through worldly abandonment. Rather than learn the true meaning of belief and its practical procedures, they become a burden on society by depriving themselves of opportunities to advance their lives. Others pursue the opposite extreme—they move away from religion and get absorbed in the material pleasures of life such that asceticism is tasteless and sometimes unbearable. It is worth noting that money and material pleasures are instruments of this world, and lives restricted to their pursuit ultimately lead to boredom, depression, and aimlessness. As it addresses this issue of immoderation, this rare piece of advice can guarantee happiness for any young person who commits him or herself to following and implementing it.

Jurists and the Media

A question commonly posed by people, particularly youth, is why supreme religious authorities like His Eminence Sayyid al-Sistani (may God prolong his life) do not appear in the media to give their advice and instructions directly to their followers and emulators. The suggestion being that this medium would be more effective and surely would strengthen the relationship between the leader and his followers. Therefore, they ask why this advice was not broadcast live via television and the Internet.

This question ignores certain basic principles of how humans are guided. It arises from the fact that people have become accustomed to seeing political leaders on television screens every day. However, prominent religious scholars, particularly those in the highest ranks of spiritual and religious leadership, do not need to appear in the media to carry out their important duties unless special circumstances necessitate such appearances.

Oftentimes, appearing in the media for one occasion leads to or necessitates having to appear for other occasions too, which can be a slippery slope. Persistent appearances in the media damage the stature of jurists and scholars and decrease the amount of attention people pay to their speeches. Hence, a jurist does not appear in the media and does not speak in public unless it is necessary. Yet when he says something, the ripples of those words can be felt across the globe. This fact should be understood by those who pose this question.

Regular appearance in the media is a requirement for those with executive and administrative jobs, as the events of daily life dictate them to communicate their opinions and decisions about public issues and events to their constituents. However, religious scholars, particularly prominent jurists, rarely need to appear and speak in public. In fact, some prominent leaders of religious seminaries and deans of well-known universities have never appeared in the media.

Dealing with today's media can be very challenging because each news organization presents the news differently and sometimes with their own interpretation of its significance (e.g., by using "experts" who comment on a particular story). It has also become inherent that each station races to be the first to break the news. This tendency of news organizations has the potential to rapidly change the course of events as they are unfolding on any given day, which can then affect the lives of people and sometimes cause negative repercussions that are much harder to repair later. Thus, caution is necessary when dealing with the media today. A person who has religious responsibility and is trusted by society has to be very cautious and careful not to cause confusion and distress, even if inadvertently. Thus, it is easy to understand why jurists, as the trustees of the prophets on religion, need to be much more cautious. A jurist always needs to think about all the consequences and all those who are impacted before uttering a word.

Therefore, we ask the dear believers and loyal followers who yearn to see and listen to the grand religious authorities through the media to take these risks into consideration and understand the circumstances surrounding them that compel them to take such precautions in order to protect the interests of all believers. In fact, the stories told by the believers who have visited the religious authorities in their residences are proof of how glad the latter are to see the believers and speak with them. It is not uncommon to hear the words 'effusive love,' 'humility,' and 'hospitality' when describing those encounters. Therefore, it should be understood that the absence of religious authorities from the media is because of these risks and circumstances not because they are insensitive to the needs of believers.

How to Communicate With Religious Authorities

Without a doubt, communication between believers and their spiritual leadership is necessary. A religious authority dedicates his life to delivering the message of the prophets and messengers in its original form to people so that the process of conveying God's message to His servants is continuous. Life during the era of prophecy and for a long time thereafter was simple. The Prophet (may God's blessings be upon him and his progeny) used to sit in the mosque and receive visitors every day. History also tells us about the most recognized teacher of Islamic disciplines from the progeny of the Prophet (may peace be upon them). Imam Jafar al-Sadiq (may peace be upon him), who was known for his lectures to scholars and researchers, followed in the tradition of his third great grandfather (i.e., the Prophet) by sitting in the Prophet's mosque in Medina and receiving and guiding laymen who asked him for advice and instruction and took comfort in his friendly manner.

However, modern life and what we encounter today is much more complex. The population is much larger, people can travel more easily, scientific disciplines have branched out and multiplied in number, the social and political conditions have become more complicated, and security risks have grown. This has made the job of religious authorities more difficult, and for this reason they have become more cautious. Indeed, these circumstances have deprived the believers of the simple life that existed during the era of the Prophet and the purified imams (may God's blessings be upon them all).

Despite all of this, the issue does not seem irresolvable. Various channels of communication are available for believers to use to interact with religious authorities, jurists, and heads of religious seminaries. When the religious authority wants to communicate a message to believers, he handwrites it and seals it with his official seal. At other times, his office makes announcements on its official website. There are also official representatives of the religious authority at his liaison offices around the world who explain his opinion, religious edicts, instructions, and advice. In regard to meeting religious authorities, despite their limited availability due to their engagement in important issues, they have always found time to receive visitors from around the world. Some religious authorities even dedicate a morning period and an evening period to meet visitors.

Therefore, we encourage all the dear believers, particularly the youth, to make regular trips to the Middle

East to visit the shrines of the holy imams (may peace be upon them) and to stop by and meet with the religious authorities, jurists, and lecturers in the religious seminaries. They can also benefit from visiting various archeological sites to become more acquainted with their culture, heritage, and history which spans thousands of years.

I.M.A.M.

Acknowledgements

Dear reader, before you is a precise, practical jurisprudence rules booklet that seeks to provide guidance to Muslims living in the West. We would like to thank and send our sincere appreciation to all those who have contributed in the preparation and processing of the materials needed to bring this booklet to light. We specifically would like to thank everyone who has written, reviewed, translated, edited, and published this content from both staff and volunteers who are part of this blessed association, I.M.A.M. May Allah reward them for their great efforts.

This booklet was translated and reviewed by Mohamed-Ridha Banoon and Dr. Haj Mehdi Saeed Hazari.

I.M.A.M.

The Request

In the name of God,
the Beneficent, the Merciful

The best of greetings to the highest religious authority, His Eminence Grand Ayatullah Sayyid Ali al-Husayni al-Sistani,

We are a group of young college students and social activists. We would like to ask Your Eminence for advice that can be useful to us in this day and age, describing the role of the youth and what is required of them to play that role. Other advice that would be beneficial to the youth is also appreciated.

[Signed] A group of college students and social activists

The Response

In the name of God,
the Beneficent, the Merciful

All praise belongs to God, Lord of
the Worlds, and may peace and
blessings be upon Muhammad
and his pure progeny.

Peace be upon you, and the mercy
of God, as well as His blessings.

I would like to give to the youth, who are immeasurably dear to me and about whom I care just as I do for myself and my family, eight principles to live by, which will provide them with happiness in this world and in the hereafter. These principles are the essence of God's message to His creation and the advice of His wise and pious servants, as well as what I have extracted from years of experience and acquiring knowledge.

First It is imperative to have true conviction and belief in God and the hereafter. Never neglect this belief under any circumstance, for it is proven by clear [rational] evidence and also decreed by the upright faith. Just observe, and you will notice, for if a person could explore the depths of every creature in this world, each time they would see a novel and unique creation that attests to a maker [creator] who is both omnipotent and mighty. As such, God's messages have come to us continuously and without interruption through His prophets to remind humankind of this fact and to indicate that this life, as He planned it, is an arena in which He tests His servants to see who is best in conduct. Thus, a person who is oblivious to the existence of God and the hereafter will not know the meaning of this life, its all-encompassing scope, and its eventual consequence [in the hereafter], and therein will be walking in darkness. Therefore, preserve and maintain your conviction and belief, and make it the most important and precious of your belongings. In fact, strive to increase your certainty [in God] through growing conviction, ensure that it never leaves you, and preserve it with deep foresight and penetrating vision.

If you experience a weakness in your faith during the prime of your youth, which might occur when feeling burdened by a religious obligation [e.g., fasting, paying khums, etc.] or are tempted by an impermissible pleasure, do not completely sever your relationship with God [by totally neglecting His commandments], because that will make it harder for you to return. One may arrogantly and purposely refuse to obey God's commands during periods of health and strength, yet eventually one will be forced to cower and go back to the Lord when afflicted with weakness and disability. Therefore, remind yourself during the periods when you are healthy and strong, which are often very short, that the times of weakness, decay, ailment, and aging are approaching and inevitable.

Beware of slipping into a constant doubt about the proven principles [of Islam] in order to justify the validity of your wrong conduct and behavior, whereby you (a) pursue ambiguities that you never took the time to analyze patiently and disprove, (b) place your trust in immature thoughts, (c) become allured by life's pleasures and vanities, or (d) resent the exploitation of religion by some people who use it for their personal interest [resulting in weakening of your adherence to the proven principles of Islam]. The measuring stick of truth is not people. Instead, people are measured by the truth.

Second Have good morals and character, because in doing so, you engender a great many excellent qualities like wisdom, consideration, kindness, modesty, frugality, prudence, patience, and others; because they are the most important reasons behind the happiness of this world and the hereafter. As such, the closest people to God, the Glorified, and the ones with the most significant deeds that tip the scale towards overwhelming good are the ones with the best morals. Therefore, improve your conduct with your parents, family, children, friends, and all people. If you find deficiencies in yourself, do not overlook them. Instead, hold yourself accountable, and carry yourself with prudence toward good morals. If you find yourself unable to behave morally, do not lose hope. Rather, force yourself to behave morally, because one who sincerely strives to be like the good people is considered one of them and will be rewarded more [for their effort] than a person who finds it already in their nature to behave in this manner.

Third Try to learn a professional trade and acquire a specialty, and exert yourself and work hard in its pursuit. This is a blessed endeavor because it allows you to occupy a portion of your free time, support yourself and your family, benefit society, perform good deeds using the money you earn, sharpen your mind, and broaden your experience. As a result, your wealth becomes more blessed because the more effort you expend in earning a livelihood, the more blessed and pleasant it is. Furthermore, God, the Glorified and Almighty, loves hardworking people who exert themselves to work and earn a livelihood and dislikes idle people who spend their time in play and diversion and are dependent [and burdensome] on others. So do not allow your youth to pass without learning a professional trade or specialty, because God has made a person's youth full of physical and psychological vigor so that he or she can acquire the skills and assets needed for the rest of their life. Thus, do not waste it in distractions and negligence.

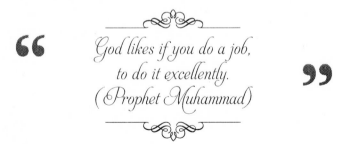

"
*God likes if you do a job,
to do it excellently.
(Prophet Muhammad)*
"

Attend to your vocation and specialty until you become proficient in it. Do not speak without knowledge, and do not practice without [first gaining] experience. If you do not know or cannot do something, acknowledge your ineptitude and apologize to your clients or customers, or refer them to those more experienced than you. This increases your credibility in their eyes. Do your work with interest, attention, and enjoyment; do not make it your goal to just collect money, especially through impermissible means, because there is no blessing in wealth acquired from prohibited sources. Be advised that a person who acquires wealth from impermissible sources is prone to adversity sent to them by God, which will result in them not only toiling and facing adversity but also parting with that money. Such wealth does not make one rich in this life and becomes a curse in the afterlife.

Make yourself the scale in your conduct with others. Consider them in place of yourself so that your conduct with them is like what you do for yourself and what you would like others to do for you. Be kind to people as you would like God to be kind to you. Maintain your professional ethics and conventions, and do not compromise the high quality and standard of your work such that you would be ashamed of it. Keep in mind that a professional has a duty towards the customers and clients who put their trust in them. Be a counselor to them, and never deceive them, because God, the Glorified, watches you and knows about your deeds; and He will punish you sooner or later, because cheating and betrayal are the most disgraceful of deeds and have the most dangerous results and consequences.

Physicians should pay particular attention to this advice and follow it more strictly, because they deal with people's bodies and minds. Therefore, they should not deviate from the aforementioned advice or they will face severe consequences.

God, the Glorified and Almighty, says, "Woe to the defrauders who use short measures, who, when they measure [a commodity bought] from the people, take the full measure but diminish when they measure or weigh for them. Do they not know that they will be resurrected?" (83:1–4). Furthermore, the Prophet (may God's blessings be upon him and his progeny) said, "God likes if you do a job, to do it excellently."

Furthermore, college students and professors should strive to be completely versed in their respective fields of expertise, [the fundamentals of] which are sometimes generated from other institutes of science [also], especially in the area of medicine, in order for their knowledge and treatment to be on the cutting edge of contemporary science. Moreover, they should pay attention to advancing science by staying up to date with useful scientific articles and pioneering discoveries, thereby rivaling other institutes of science in innovation as much as they can. They should not settle for being mere students of others and consumers of the tools and equipment others make. Instead, they should actively contribute to advancing science, just as their ancestors were pioneers and leaders of science in previous times. Yet, they should know that no particular generation is worthier in seeking leadership [in any field of study] than another [so you can also do the same].

Therefore, you should nurture the youth who have distinctive abilities, who possess genius, and who exhibit intelligence, excellence, and potential to succeed, even if they are from the underprivileged classes. Support them as you support your children so they may reach the pinnacle of beneficial knowledge. You will get rewarded for all they produce due to this support, and your society and offspring will benefit from them as well.

Fourth Adhere to good deeds and morals and abstain from bad ones. Prosperity and abundance arise from virtue, whereas misery and evil, except those [difficulties and challenges] used by God to test His servants, arise from vice. God, the Glorified, says,

66 *Whatever affliction that may visit you is because of what your hands have earned, and He excuses many (an offense).*
(Quran 42:30) 99

Virtuous deeds include holding oneself responsible for all the things one does, practicing chastity in appearance, gaze, and behavior, truthfulness in speech, maintaining the bonds of kinship, returning that which is entrusted, fulfilling commitments and obligations, resolve in righteousness, and disdaining vile conduct and behavior.

Vicious deeds that are abhorred include prejudice [i.e., racial, ethnic, tribal, etc.], being easily enraged, impermissible entertainment, showing off in front of people, extravagance at times of abundance, transgression at times of poverty, vexation at times of adversity, doing evil to others, particularly the weak, squandering money, lack of gratitude for God's bestowal, conceit in sin, assisting in injustice and aggression, and loving to be thanked for a deed one did not do.

I want to stress the issue of chastity regarding young, unmarried women, because women are more affected by the consequences of neglecting it due to their delicateness. Thus, let them not be deceived by false emotions, and do not enter casual relationships whose enjoyment ends quickly, but the potentially negative complications and consequences of which persist. Young, unmarried women should only think about a stable life that contains the elements of loyalty and happiness. No woman is more dignified than the one who maintains her composure and strength, who is reserved in her appearance and behavior, and who busies her time with her life, work, and studies.

Fifth Give importance to starting a family by getting married and having children without any delay. Having a family is a source of pleasure and affability, a motive for hard work, a cause for sobriety and being responsible, an investment of energy for the future, and a defense against forbidden and lowly deeds. It has been narrated that one who gets married has attained half of their religion. More importantly, marriage is a necessary course of life and a natural human instinct. Those who abandon it fall into trouble and are afflicted with monotony and laziness. Do not be afraid of becoming poor due to marriage because God, the Glorified, has put many means of sustenance in marriage that one may not be aware of at first. Also, pay attention to the character of the woman you want to marry—her piety and discipline—and do not be occupied with evaluating her beauty, her appearance, and her job, because those traits are a veil that may be removed when life reveals its hardships. There are warnings in the authentic traditions of Prophet Muhammad (pbuh) and his holy family against marrying a woman merely for her looks. Moreover, one who marries a woman for her piety and character will have a blessed marriage.

Let young, unmarried women and their guardians not favor getting a job over starting a family because marriage is a necessary part of life while a job and career are more of a complement to it. It is not wise to abandon the former for the sake of the latter. Those who do not understand this principle will regret it later in life when, unfortunately, regret will be of no help. Life's experiences attest to this.

Guardians are not permitted to prevent their daughters from getting married, nor are they permitted to put obstacles in their way using improper traditions that are not required by God, such as asking for exorbitant dowries or delaying the process of marriage so their daughters can marry cousins or sayyids, because there are many sources of corruption in these practices. God made fathers the guardians of their daughters only for the sake of counsel and ensuring the best option for them. One who prohibits a woman for reasons other than her interest has committed a sin that persists as long as she suffers [due to that unfair prohibition] and has opened one of hell's doors upon himself.

Sixth Seek opportunities to do good deeds, and strive towards giving charity and helping people, particularly orphans, widows, and the disadvantaged, and always strive for the common good. Such practices enhance your faith, discipline your soul, and purify your wealth and the gifts bestowed upon you by God. They also promote cooperation in virtue, piety, silently enjoining good and forbidding evil, assistance to the authorities in keeping order and protecting the public interest, and a means by which the betterment of society can be achieved. They are a blessing in this world and a safe-keeping for the afterlife. God, the Glorified, loves a community that lives in solidarity and cooperation, in which every person cares about the interests of others just as they care about their own interest.

> *Indeed Allah does not change a people's lot unless they change what is in their souls.*
> *(Quran 13:11)*

God says, "If the people of the towns had been faithful and God-fearing, We would have opened to them blessings from the heaven" (7:96), and He says, "Indeed Allah does not change a people's lot unless they change what is in their souls" (13:11). The Prophet (may God's blessings be upon him and his progeny) said, "One of you does not become a believer until he likes for his brother what he likes for himself and dislikes for his brother what he dislikes for himself," and also said, "One who establishes a good tradition gets rewarded for it and also for those who follow that tradition."

Seventh Attend to the responsibilities you have assumed, whether towards your family or society. Let fathers attend to their children and husbands attend to their wives. Abstain from violence and cruelty even when there is a need for strictness to preserve the family and society. The ways of being strict are not limited to bodily injury and distasteful remarks. There are other means and approaches of discipline that can be learned from experts and specialists. Indeed, cruel measures often result in the opposite of what is intended. They cause a bad condition to take deeper root and have an opposite effect of what is intended in the person whom they are supposed to reform. There is no good in strictness that causes injustice, and a mistake cannot be remedied with another mistake [or by committing a sin].

Let those who assume responsibilities in society discharge them appropriately. Let them be sincere counselors for the good of society and not betray its objectives, for God is the custodian of everybody, and He will call them to account on the Day of Resurrection. Therefore, do not spend public money wastefully or make decisions that harm the public. Do not exploit your position to establish a class of people who cover up for each other, who mutually share the illegal benefits and dubious monies, and who remove others from positions that they deserve or deny them services entitled to them. Treat all people equally. Do not use your public job as a means to fulfill private obligations such as those related to kinship, past favors, etc., because fulfilling private obligations with public funds is injustice and corruption. If you ever have the option to choose one over an equally qualified other, then choose the weaker one who has no sponsor and no supporter except God. Let nobody take religion or sect into consideration when working for the public good, for the true religion is based on the true principles of justice, doing good, honesty, etc. God says, "Certainly We sent Our apostles with manifest proofs, and We sent down with them the Book and the Balance, so that mankind may maintain justice" (57:25).

Also, the Imam [Ali] (may peace be upon him) said, "I heard the Prophet of God (may God's blessings be upon him and his progeny) say on various occasions, 'A nation in which the weak cannot take back their property from the strong without stuttering will not be sanctified.'" Anyone who does not follow this principle will be deceiving themselves with false wishes and hopes. The true followers of just leaders, such as the Prophet (may God's blessings be upon him and his progeny), Imam Ali (may peace be upon him), and the martyr, Imam Hussain (may peace be upon him), are those who follow their teachings and emulate their conduct. Let those who assume public responsibilities read the letter of Imam Ali (may peace be upon him) to Malik al-Ashtar upon sending him to Egypt. That letter is a complete description of the principles of justice and fidelity. It is very beneficial to governors and even people with lesser responsibilities, yet the bigger the responsibility a person has, the more binding and obligatory it is on him [to read it].

Eighth Inculcate within yourself a spirit of learning and a desire to increase your knowledge and wisdom in all stages of your life and in all conditions. Reflect on your deeds and traits and their effects, and ponder the incidents that happen around you and their results so that you become more knowledgeable and experienced every day. Indeed, there is a lesson and guidance in every act or incident, for this life is a source of learning with great vastness and endless depth, and there is a message and meaning in everything that happens. Everything that occurs reveals a message and phenomena and represents examples and lessons to those who ponder over it. Therefore, never neglect or ignore an opportunity to gain knowledge and experience until the last day of your life. The more knowledgeable a person is, the more trials and errors they will avoid. God, the Glorified, says, "and he who is given wisdom is certainly given an abundant good" (2:269), and He says to His Prophet (may God's blessings be upon him and his progeny) "and say, 'My Lord! Increase me in knowledge'" (20:114).

and he who is given wisdom is certainly given an abundant good (Quran 2:269)

Moreover, one should acquaint oneself with three books [in particular], and contemplate their messages:

FIRST AND FOREMOST IS THE QURAN. It is the final message of God to His creation. He sent this message to sharpen the minds and make springs of wisdom erupt from them, as well as soften hardened hearts.

He narrated stories in it as examples to its readers [to learn from]. One should not abandon reading this book [for one's own benefit], because in reading it, one will feel in their soul that God is talking to them. That is because God, the Almighty, sent this book as a message to the world.

THE SECOND IS *NAHJ AL-BALAGHAH.* This book further elaborates upon the themes of the Quran and its intricate messages in an eloquent style that evokes a spirit of reflection, contemplation, learning, and wisdom. Therefore, one should read it whenever one has a chance and imagine that Imam Ali (may peace be upon him) is addressing you directly. Also, one should pay special attention to the letter of Imam Ali (may peace be upon him) to his son, Imam Hassan (may peace be upon him), because it contains a similar guiding message.

THE THIRD IS *AL-SAHIFAH AL-SAJJADIYAH.* It contains eloquent supplications whose meanings are extracted from the Quran. There are teachings in those supplications about how one's orientation, obsession, vision, and ambition should be. They also teach one how to call oneself to account and how to scrutinize and criticize oneself, particularly the supplication of Makarim al-Akhlaq (Noble Moral Traits).

These eight principles are the foundation for steadfastness in life; however, I have written them only as a reminder. They are obvious because one can see them in the light of righteousness, the brilliance of truth, the purity of what is innate to human nature, the proof of reason, and the experience of life. Also, divine messages and the instructions of the enlightened have stressed them. Therefore, everyone should follow them, particularly the youth, who are in the peak of their energy and their bodily and spiritual abilities. Even if they do not follow all of them, let them know that taking a little is better than abandoning the lot, and obtaining a part is better than losing the whole. God, the Glorified, says,

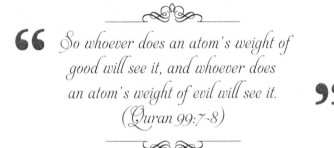

So whoever does an atom's weight of good will see it, and whoever does an atom's weight of evil will see it. (Quran 99:7-8)

I ask God to help you achieve happiness and righteousness in this life and the afterlife, as He is the Lord of Success.

Rabi al-Awwal 28, 1437 AH

Appendix

A Biography of His Eminence
Sayyid al-Sistani

Birth and Lineage

His Eminence Sayyid al-Sistani was born on the ninth of Rabi al-Awwal in 1439 AH in the Holy City of Mashhad in Iran.[4]

His father is Sayyid Muhammad Baqir, the son of Sayyid Ali al-Husayni al-Sistani (may God have mercy on them). Both were prominent and well-known scholars in the religious seminaries in Najaf, Qum, and Mashhad.

His lineage is traced to Imam Hussain ibn Ali ibn Abi Talib (may peace be upon them), the son of Fatimah, daughter of Muhammad (may God's blessings be upon them and their progeny).

---

4. Most of the information herein was taken from the official website of the office of His Eminence, www.sistani.org, with some additions and alterations.

Character

Most of the people who have known His Eminence Sayyid al-Sistani and have accompanied him have noted that, since his youth, he was a quiet person who spent most of his time in meditation and reflection. They say he has a calm, content, and patient personality. He is very humble and has lived an extremely simple life. His asceticism is apparent from his food, clothing, and residence. He does not like dissemblance and forbids his representatives from spending a penny on advertising his religious authority or posting his pictures in public places. Moreover, he does not like titles, to the extent that he has deleted the title of "Ayatullah" from some pages of his office's website. Also, he does not allow any organization or Islamic center to be named after him. Instead, he instructs believers to name them after historic scholars in order to resurrect their names and keep them in memory. Finally, there is his fatherly spirit. He does not favor a person over another, whatever their color, language, ethnicity, or status. He considers himself a father to all believers—needing to be fair and just in treating them all.

Scholarly Journey

His Eminence started learning the Quran and reading and writing at the age of five years. He started studying religious disciplines by the beginning of the second decade of his life and continued until he attended the doctrinal lectures of Ayatullah Mirza Mahdi al-Ashtiani and the jurisprudential research lectures of Ayatullah Mirza Hashim al-Qazwini in Mashhad.

He moved to the religious seminary in Qum in 1368 AH and attended the research lectures of the supreme religious authority, Sayyid Hussain al-Tabatabai al-Burujirdi (may God have mercy on him), on jurisprudence and its roots. He also learned much about the disciplines of hadith and biographical evaluation from him. In addition, he attended the lectures of the great jurisprudent, Sayyid Muhammad al-Hujjah al-Kuhkamari (may God have mercy on him).

He decamped to the religious seminary in Najaf at the beginning of the year 1371 AH and has resided there ever since. He attended the research lectures on jurisprudence and its roots given by the two prominent figures Sayyid Abu al-Qasim al-Musawi al-Khui and Shaykh Hussain al-Hilli (may God have mercy on them) and accompanied them for a long period of time. During that time, he also attended the research lectures of other prominent figures including Sayyid Muhsin al-Hakim and Sayyid Mahmud al-Shahrudi (may God have mercy on them).

He outshined his peers through wit, ample research, perseverance in learning, and familiarity with various theories in different religious disciplines, thereby becoming in 1381 AH the only one among his peers (i.e., the scholars in the early thirties) to receive the following certificates from prominent scholars:

- Certificate of absolute ijtihad from his master, His Eminence Sayyid al-Khui (may God have mercy on him), who did not give such a certificate to anyone except him and Shaykh Ali al-Falsafi

- Certificate of absolute ijtihad from his master, Shaykh Hussain al-Hilli, who did not issue such a certificate to anyone other than His Eminence

- A certificate from the greatest of muhaddiths, Shaykh Agha Buzurg al-Tehrani, commending His Eminence's skill in the disciplines of hadith and biographical evaluation. The certificate was dated 1380 AH.

He taught jurisprudential research beginning in 1381 AH and roots of jurisprudence research beginning in 1384 AH. However, deteriorating security conditions have compelled him to stop lecturing in recent years.

He has authored more than forty published and unpublished works. A complete list of them can be found on the website of His Eminence's office, may God prolong his life.

Features of His Eminence's School of Thought

His Eminence cares about knowing the roots of the jurisprudential question and its surrounding circumstances, including the doctrinal and political environment, before issuing his jurisprudential verdict. Thus, he does not limit himself to religious texts only.

He connects seminary thought to contemporary culture. The reason is that a question may take many manifestations, requiring the jurisprudent to know all the schools of thought and what makes them have different opinions and interpretations of the same issue.

He is committed to the principle of modernization in the theories and premises of jurisprudence and its roots and does not settle for discussing the existing literature and commenting on it. Take the principle of respect as an example. It is the principle of respecting others and their opinions and laws. His Eminence modernized this great Islamic principle and formulated it as a jurisprudential code used by believers who live in non-Muslim or mixed, multi-religious countries.

He is committed to the comparative study of the different schools of great religious seminaries, using the opinions of their most prominent jurisprudents. For example, he mentions the opinion of Sayyid al-Burujirdi as a representative of the school of Qum; then he mentions the opinions of Sayyid al-Khui and Shaykh Hussain al-Hilli as representatives of the school of Najaf; then he compares and analyzes those opinions before finally giving his own opinion. He does the same when discussing issues in which the jurisprudents of the Shia Imami school have a different opinion than that of the jurisprudents of other Islamic schools.

He is thoroughly aware of other disciplines and specialties, such as contemporary law. For example, he examines French, Egyptian, and Iraqi laws and employs them in analyzing jurisprudential principles and expanding their use.

Religious Authority

His Eminence was among the most distinguished students of the Supreme Religious Authority, Sayyid al-Khui (may God have mercy on him) (1413 AH), as he was the only one of his students to give research lectures during his life. His master paid special attention to his abilities and even appointed him to be the imam of congregational prayer at al-Khadra Mosque.[5] After the passing away of Sayyid al-Khui, Sayyid al-Gulpaygani (may God have mercy on him) of Qum and Sayyid Abd al-Ala al-Sabzawari (may God have mercy on him) of Najaf emerged as religious authorities. However, both of them passed away shortly (1414 AH). After them, Shaykh Muhammad Ali al-Araki and Sayyid Muhammad al-Ruhani (may God have mercy on them) emerged as religious authorities. Nevertheless, they passed away in a short period of time too. Consequently, people in religious and seminary circles looked upon His Eminence Sayyid al-Sistani (may God prolong his life) because of his high religious stature and his piety and prudence. Several prominent jurisprudents, such

---

5. Al-Khadra Mosque is a historical mosque adjacent to the shrine of the Leader of the Faithful, may peace be upon him. It has a high symbolic status. For years, only supreme religious authorities led congregational prayers in it and lectured there.

as His Eminence Ayatullah Sayyid Ali al-Bihishti and His Eminence Ayatullah Murtada al-Burujirdi in addition to many senior lecturers in the seminaries of Qum and Najaf, directed believers to emulate Sayyid al-Sistani. As a result, many believers in Iraq, Iran, the Gulf, Pakistan, and India started to emulate His Eminence. Soon, most believers in other Muslim and non-Muslim countries around the world were emulating him. To this day, he is the supreme religious authority who has the most emulators among believers. May the Almighty prolong his life and help Islam and Muslims with his existence.

Struggle and Important Events

His Eminence resisted the plan of the Baathist regime to suppress the religious seminary with the highest degree of patience and forbearance. The Baathist regime expelled many jurisprudents and scholars, including some of His Eminence Sayyid al-Sistani's students. His Eminence himself was on the verge of being expelled several times. He was questioned more than once and tolerated the insults and offenses of the Baathists. However, all that pressure could not change his decision not to leave the religious seminary in Najaf.

He tolerated and resisted the pressure and harassment of the Baathist regime during the Iran-Iraq war. When Iraqi people revolted in 1411 AH and the regime crushed the revolution with brute force, it detained His Eminence Sayyid al-Sistani and many other scholars.

They were persecuted, harshly questioned, and even tortured in the notorious Ridhwaniyah detention camp. The Baathist regime later assassinated some of them such as Martyr Ayatullah Shaykh Murtada al-Burujirdi and Martyr Ayatullah Mirza Ali al-Gharawi.

After the passing away of the Supreme Religious Authority Sayyid al-Khui (may God be pleased with him) and the acceptance of His Eminence Sayyid al-Sistani as a religious authority, the Baathist regime pressed to change the direction of the religious authority in Najaf. It did what it could to tarnish the reputation of Sayyid al-Sistani and damage his stature among jurisprudents and used various methods to not let believers meet him, such as closing al-Khadra Mosque in 1414 AH. When all those attempts failed, the regime planned to assassinate him, as documents recovered after the fall of the Baath regime show.[6] As a result, he stayed in his house for several years and could not even visit the shrine of the Leader of the Faithful (may peace be upon him) although his house was only a few meters from the shrine.

After the fall of the Baathist regime and the occupation of Iraq in 1424 AH (2003 CE), the occupiers attempted to dictate a certain constitution and system of government

---

6. "The Hawza under Siege," by Dr. Abbas Kadhim, Boston University. Online PDF file available on:
http://www.bu.edu/iis/files/2013/04/ Bath-Party-ArchiveFinal-1.pdf

to Iraqis. In response, His Eminence Sayyid al-Sistani (may God prolong his life) sent a letter to the Security Council warning of the risks of approving the so-called transitional law. The Security Council complied with the request of His Eminence. Also, he issued his famous edict insisting that only Iraqis draft the new constitution, that there be a referendum on the constitution so that Iraqis decide whether or not it takes effect, and that the constitution not be in conflict with Islamic principles and the noble values of the Iraqi people.[7] In the end, that was what happened, and the system of government in the new Iraq was in compliance with the opinion of the supreme religious authority, embodied in His Eminence Grand Ayatullah Sayyid al-Sistani (may God prolong his life). Therefore, he not only protected Iraq from being dominated by the occupiers but contributed to protecting the entire region from a grand plan for which the occupation of Iraq was only the beginning.

His Eminence Sayyid al-Sistani left Iraq on the nineteenth of Shaban 1425 AH (August 6, 2004) to have a heart surgery in one of London's hospitals. His absence encouraged various local and foreign parties to exploit the resulting power vacuum and its psychological effects on the political situation. As a result, violence broke out in Iraq and warring factions entered even the holy shrine of Imam Ali (may peace be upon him) and used it as a base. This exposed Najaf to shelling and

---

7. The edict can be found on the website of the office of His Eminence Sayyid al-Sistani:
http://www.sistani.org/arabic/archive/273/

destruction and the holy shrine was on the verge of being destroyed. At that time, the medical authorities in the British hospital permitted His Eminence to leave the hospital. He immediately left and boarded the first plane going to Kuwait. Upon landing in Kuwait, he headed directly to Basra. Then he joined millions of believers in a grand march from Basra to Najaf. Despite all the risks and the possibility of a disaster threatened by some parties in the war, His Eminence (may God prolong his life) insisted on liberating Najaf from warfare, whatever the price. His Eminence arrived in Najaf with millions accompanying him on the ninth of Rajab. Upon seeing millions marching toward them, the warring parties left the holy shrine. As such, His Eminence prevented a catastrophe that would have irreparably damaged the dignity and status of the Imami school of Islam.

As a result of the fall of the Baathist regime and the occupation, Iraq witnessed unusual waves of politicized sectarian fighting. Frantic campaigns of identity-based killing started. Leaders of aberration, along with commanders of some factions, helped this sectarian unrest with funds, weapons, and propaganda until it reached such a high degree that the holy shrine of the two Askari imams in Samarra was detonated on the twenty-third of Muharram 1427 AH. The entire country was on the verge of explosion, and the Tigris and Euphrates rivers were at risk of being colored red with blood. His Eminence employed his wisdom and shrewdness and the highest degree of restraint despite all the tragedies and atrocities he was witnessing.

He issued religious edicts and instructions to forbid assaulting any human being, whether they be Muslim or non-Muslim, a Shia or a Sunni. He repeated his famous saying, "Do not say, 'Our brothers, the Sunnis,' but say, 'Ourselves.'" He forbade seizing the mosques of one sect by another and pressured zealots to leave the mosques they had seized although those mosques were in their areas. As such, he was able to stop the sectarian war and return peace and security to Iraq and its people. However, it should be noted that attempts to reignite sectarian war in Iraq have not stopped.

Last but not least is the historical religious edict of collective jihad[8] on the eleventh of Shaban 1435 AH against the terrorist group ISIS, which crossed the border overnight and occupied Mosul and reached as far as a few kilometers from Baghdad amid a complete collapse of the Iraqi army and high treason by its leadership in the area. Immediately, thousands of believers volunteered to become soldiers under the command of the Iraqi army, obeying the order issued by His Eminence (may God prolong his life) as he refused to let them fight under the command of any entity except the official Iraqi army. This religious edict was a first, coming approximately 100 years after the edict of jihad against the British occupiers of Iraq in 1920 CE. As a result, Iraq and the region were prevented from falling under the control of the Khawarij of our time and

---

8. The edict can be found on the website of the office of His Eminence Sayyid al-Sistani:
http://www.sistani.org/arabic/statement/24906/

the leaders of aberration. We ask God, the Glorified, to protect believers and their homelands from the evil of their enemies embodied in al-Qaeda, Taliban, ISIS, the Nusra, and other groups and to expedite the return of our master, Sahib al-Zaman (may peace be upon him), who will spread justice and equity in this world after it is filled with injustice and inequity.

His Eminence Sayyid al-Sistani is the first religious authority to be commended by the Security Council of the United Nations for his role in combating terrorism and his sponsorship of displaced Sunni Muslims, Christians, and other minorities who emigrated to Najaf and Karbala after the brutal assault of the terrorist gang ISIS. That commendation came in the Security Council report issued on January 10, 2014.[9] His Eminence is also the first religious authority whom a Secretary-General of the United Nations visited in his residence to thank him and appreciate his efforts and positions against extremism and terror. On July 24, 2014 the Secretary-General of the United Nations visited His Eminence Sayyid al-Sistani and spoke with him for about an hour. He expressed his appreciation of the position of Sayyid al-Sistani that calls for peace and preserving the unity of the country. He said, "I am extremely honored to have met His Eminence Grand Ayatollah Al-Sistani today for the first time. He is a man of the deepest wisdom and tolerance. He is an inspiration and a role model for his many followers in Iraq and beyond."

---

9. http://www.un.org/apps/news/story.asp?NewsID=46909&Cr=Iraq&Cr1=#.VwigrEfko1p

He added, "I expressed the United Nations' gratitude for His Eminence's support for all efforts to protect civilians in the current conflict...I expressed to His Eminence how deeply moved I was by his consistent calls for all sides to refrain from sectarian or ethnic rhetoric." The Secretary-General Ban Ki-Moon ended his remarks by saying, "Once again, I was deeply impressed by my time with His Eminence. You can continue to count on my full support along with the United Nations as the people of Najaf and all of Iraq work to build a tolerant, peaceful, and prosperous country for all its people."[10]

10. http://www.un.org/sg/offthecuff/index.asp?nid=3496

Other publications from I.M.A.M.

Available for purchase online

- ❖ Who Is Hussain?
  by Dr. Mehdi Saeed Hazari

- ❖ The Illuminating Lantern:
  An Exposition of Subtleties from the Quran
  by Shaykh Habib al-Kadhimi

- ❖ Fasting: A Haven from Hellfire
  by Grand Ayatullah Sayyid Ali al-Sistani

- ❖ Tajwid: A Guide to Qur'anic Recitation
  by Shaykh Rizwan Arastu

- ❖ God's Emissaries: Adam to Jesus
  by Shaykh Rizwan Arastu